◆ **Hispanic Headliners** ◆

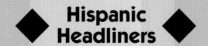

Mark Sanchez

Quarterback on the Rise

Zella Williams

PowerKiDS press.

New York

Published in 2011 by The Rosen Publishing Group, Inc.
29 East 21st Street, New York, NY 10010

First Edition

Editor: Joanne Randolph
Book Design: Kate Laczynski
Photo Researcher: Jessica Gerweck

Photo Credits: Cover, p. 1 Jim Luzzi/Getty Images; pp. 4, 13 (top) Joe Robbins/Getty Images; pp. 5, 22 Scott Boehm/Getty Images; p. 6 Ben Liebenberg/Getty Images; pp. 7, 14, 15, 16, 17, 20 Al Pereira/Getty Images; pp. 8, 11 © Danny Moloshok/Icon SMI; pp. 9, 10 © Juliann Tallino/Maxpreps/Icon SMI; p. 12 Tom Hauck/Getty Images; p. 13 (bottom) Christian Petersen/Getty Images; pp. 18–19 Jim Rogash/Getty Images; p. 21 Andy Lyons/Getty Images.

Library of Congress Cataloging-in-Publication Data
Williams, Zella.
  Mark Sanchez : quarterback on the rise / Zella Williams. — 1st ed.
     p. cm. — (Hispanic headliners)
  Includes index.
  ISBN 978-1-4488-1459-6 (library binding) — ISBN 978-1-4488-1484-8 (pbk.) — ISBN 978-1-4488-1485-5 (6-pack)
  1. Sanchez, Mark—Juvenile literature. 2. Football players—United States—Biography—Juvenile literature. 3. Quarterbacks (Football—United States—Biography—Juvenile literature. I. Title.
  GV939.S175W55 2011
  796.332092—dc22
  [B]
                                          2010010502

Manufactured in the United States of America

CPSIA Compliance Information: Batch #WS10PK: For Further Information contact Rosen Publishing, New York, New York at 1-800-237-9932

CONTENTS

Are you a football fan? If you are, you may have heard of Mark Sanchez. He was an award-winning college football player. He then became the New York Jets' starting quarterback in 2009. He is known for his

Here Mark Sanchez practices throwing the football to one of his teammates.

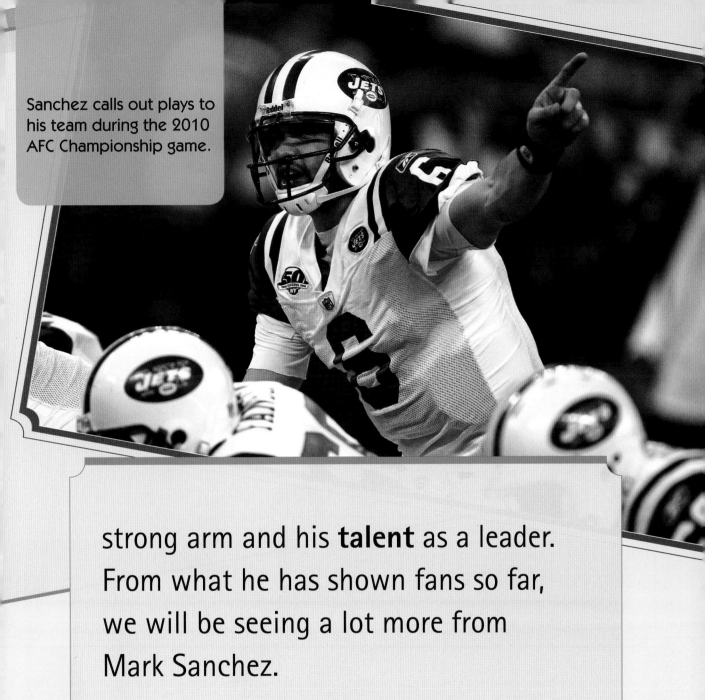

Sanchez calls out plays to his team during the 2010 AFC Championship game.

strong arm and his **talent** as a leader. From what he has shown fans so far, we will be seeing a lot more from Mark Sanchez.

Mark Sanchez was born on November 11, 1986, in Long Beach, California. His parents were Nick and Olga Sanchez, who are both Mexican Americans. After his parents **divorced**, he and his brothers, Nick Jr.

Mark and Nick Sanchez stand together outside Mark's old high school.

and Brandon, moved with their father to Rancho Santa Margarita. The boys spent part of their time with each parent.

Nick Sanchez pushed his sons to work hard at their studies. He pushed them to be leaders. He also made sure they played sports. Both of Mark's older brothers played

All of Sanchez's hard work paid off when he became the quarterback on his high-school team.

Sanchez is shown here in 2004 playing in a championship game for his high school.

football in high school and college. Mark had the most talent as an athlete. He trained hard to become quarterback on his high-school team.

Mark Sanchez went to Santa Margarita High School. He started playing football in his second year. In 2003, before his third year started, he moved to a different high school. He played basketball, baseball, and

Sanchez is trying to stop the player in the center from tackling him so that he can throw the ball.

Sanchez stands in his Mission Viejo High School uniform here.

football at Mission Viejo High School. While on the football team there, he led the Diablos to a championship game.

Mark Sanchez won many honors as a high-school quarterback. In 2005, he went to the University of Southern California and played college

Part of a quarterback's job is to direct the plays the team makes.

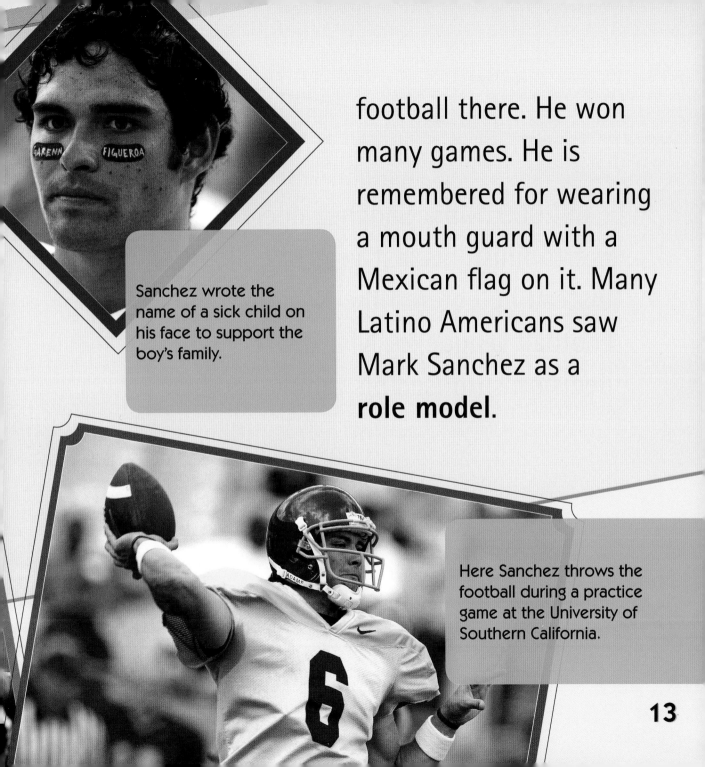

football there. He won many games. He is remembered for wearing a mouth guard with a Mexican flag on it. Many Latino Americans saw Mark Sanchez as a **role model**.

Sanchez wrote the name of a sick child on his face to support the boy's family.

Here Sanchez throws the football during a practice game at the University of Southern California.

In 2009, Mark Sanchez decided not to finish his last year of college. Instead he entered the National Football League, or NFL, **draft**. His **decision** surprised his family and his

Here Mark Sanchez talks with a reporter at the 2009 NFL Draft.

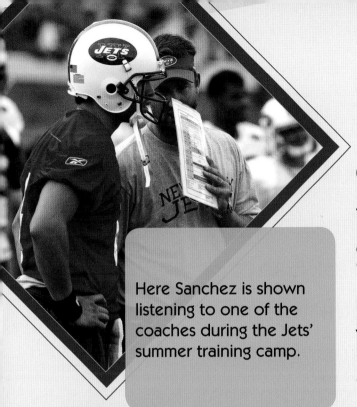

Here Sanchez is shown listening to one of the coaches during the Jets' summer training camp.

coaches. His coaches tried to get him to stay. Sanchez had made up his mind, though. The New York Jets drafted him in the first round.

Jets owner Woody Johnson talked with the press after the Jets drafted Sanchez. They hold up his team jersey.

Training camp for the Jets 2009 season started that spring. Mark Sanchez was listed as the second quarterback at the start of camp. By August 26, though, he had moved up to the starting spot. He

Mark Sanchez is getting ready to throw the ball during a practice game here.

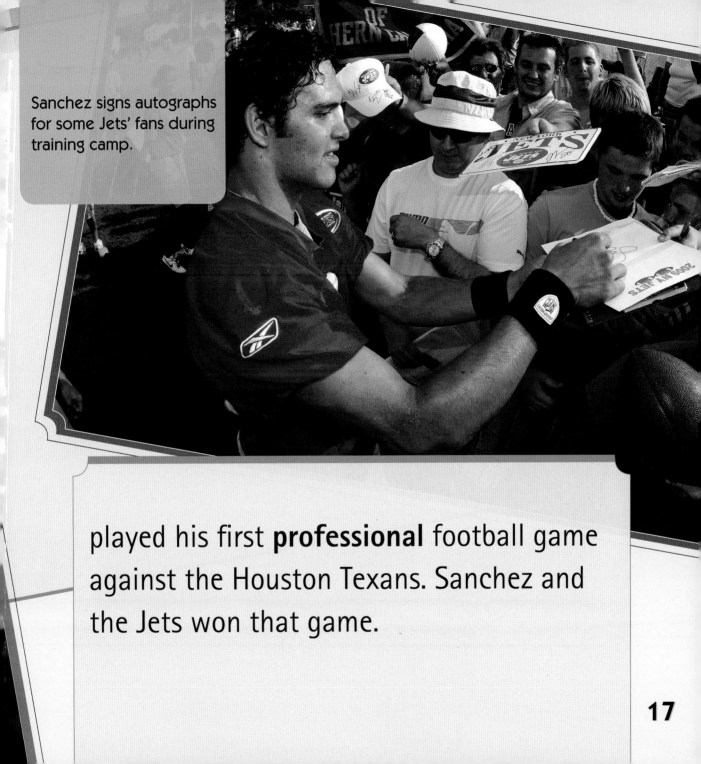

Sanchez signs autographs for some Jets' fans during training camp.

played his first **professional** football game against the Houston Texans. Sanchez and the Jets won that game.

The win against the Texans was the first of many for Mark Sanchez. He won the first three games of his **rookie** season. Sanchez was picked as the Rookie Player of the Week for each

Here Mark Sanchez is shown playing in his first home game as a New York Jet.

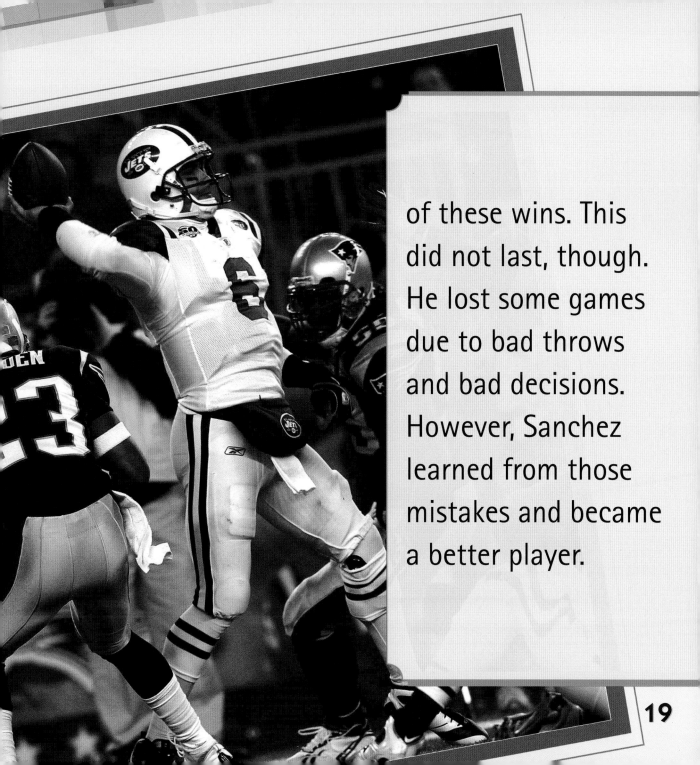

of these wins. This did not last, though. He lost some games due to bad throws and bad decisions. However, Sanchez learned from those mistakes and became a better player.

While Sanchez did not win every game, he still played well. In fact, he led the Jets to the play-offs. After winning two games, the team went on to the AFC Championship game. "AFC" stands for "American

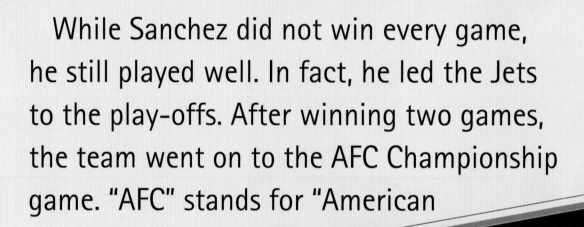

Sanchez was the fourth rookie quarterback ever to make it to an AFC Championship game.

Mark Sanchez is shown here fighting off a tackle during the 2010 AFC Championship game.

Football Conference." The Jets did not win this game, but it was still a great season for a rookie quarterback!

Mark Sanchez is just starting his NFL career. He has the talent and leadership skills to go a long way. Most quarterbacks want to lead their teams to the

Super Bowl. Mark Sanchez wants the same thing. Do you think he can do it? Keep your eyes on this young Mexican-American athlete. He is a star quarterback on the rise!

GLOSSARY

decision (dih-SIH-zhun) The choice a person makes.

divorced (dih-VORSD) Ended a marriage legally.

draft (DRAFT) The picking of people for a special purpose.

professional (pruh-FESH-nul) Someone who is paid for what he or she does.

role model (ROHL MAH-dul) A person other people want to be like, or a hero.

rookie (RU-kee) A new professional sports player.

talent (TA-lent) Skill.

INDEX

A
athlete, 9, 22

C
college, 9, 12, 14

D
decision(s), 14, 19

F
fan(s), 4–5
football, 4, 9–11, 13

G
game(s), 11, 13, 17–21

H
high school, 9–11

L
leader(s), 5, 8
Long Beach, California, 6

P
parent(s), 6–7

R
Rancho Santa Margarita, California, 7
role model, 13

S
Sanchez, Brandon (brother), 6–8
Sanchez, Nick (father), 6–8
Sanchez, Nick Jr. (brother), 6, 8
Sanchez, Olga (mother), 6
season, 16, 18, 21
sports, 8
studies, 8

T
talent, 5, 9, 22
team(s), 9, 11, 20, 22

WEB SITES

Due to the changing nature of Internet links, PowerKids Press has developed an online list of Web sites related to the subject of this book. This site is updated regularly. Please use this link to access the list:
www.powerkidslinks.com/hh/sanchez/